A Catechism... for Kids

Fr. Kris D. Stubna
Mike Aquilina

Our Sunday Visitor Publishing Division
Our Sunday Visitor, Inc.
Huntington, Indiana 46750

Nihil Obstat:
Reverend James Wehner, S.T.D.
Imprimatur:
✠ William J. Winter, V.G., S.T.D.
Auxiliary Bishop and Vicar General
Diocese of Pittsburgh
May 29, 2001

The *Nihil Obstat* and *Imprimatur* are official declarations that a book or pamphlet is free from doctrinal or moral error. It is not implied that those who have granted the *Nihil Obstat* and *Imprimatur* agree with the contents, opinions, or statements expressed. Scripture texts used in this work may be verbatim or paraphrased and are taken from the *New American Bible With Revised New Testament*, copyright © 1986, 1970 by the Confraternity of Christian Doctrine, Inc., and from the *Revised Standard Version, Catholic Edition*, copyright © 1965 and 1966 by the Division of Christian Education of the National Council of Churches of Christ in the U.S.A. The text of this work is based on the teaching of the *Catechism of the Catholic Church, Second Edition*, for use in the United States of America, copyright © 1994 and 1997, United States Catholic Conference — Libreria Editrice Vaticana. Every reasonable effort has been made to determine copyright holders and to secure permissions as needed. If any copyrighted materials have been inadvertently used without proper credit being given in one manner or another, please notify Our Sunday Visitor in writing so that future editions may be corrected accordingly.

ISBN: 0-87973-722-0
LCCCN: 2001-132450

Cover design by Monica Haneline
Interior design by Sherri L. Hoffman

Interior art reprinted from *Clip Art for Year C*, art by Steve Erspamer. Copyright © 1994, Archdiocese of Chicago, Liturgy Training Publications, 1800 N. Hermitage Ave., Chicago, IL 60622

PRINTED IN THE UNITED STATES OF AMERICA

*Dedicated to our parents,
who taught us the Catholic Faith,
sometimes using words.*

TABLE OF CONTENTS

PREFACE

As we enter the Third Millennium of Grace, we are aware of the great hunger among many, especially our young people, for some meaning and direction in life which begin with an introduction to Christ. The *Catechism of the Catholic Church* addresses the need to share, at every level of catechesis and in a variety of ways, the content of our Catholic Faith. This satisfying of the hunger for God begins with the spiritual food of our Faith, which is so well articulated in the *Catechism*. Father Kris Stubna and Mike Aquilina have taken the challenge and provide a rich source of spiritual nourishment in *A Pocket Catechism for Kids*.

Here we find in a concise and easily recognized and remembered fashion the essential elements of the Faith presented for young people. Most particularly attractive about *A Pocket Catechism for Kids* is the format of question and answer to the many inquiries that continually arise as people attempt to grow more deeply in their understanding of the Faith. Enriching the work is "A Treasury of Prayers" with its collection of beloved and well-used Catholic prayers.

As we move into the new millennium with its emphasis on evangelization — an outreach that includes sharing the Faith with so many of our young people — the questions that naturally arise will find initial answers in this handy, trustworthy catechetical tool. The authors have done all of us involved in catechesis a service by making available this useful introduction to the Faith.

In recommending *A Pocket Catechism for Kids*, I also ask God's blessings on those who use it in the catechetical effort to help achieve the new evangelization that carries with it so much hope for the future of the

Church as we attempt here and now to manifest God's kingdom.

✠ *Donald W. Wuerl*
Bishop of Pittsburgh

INTRODUCTION

Once, a long time ago, a man stumbled upon a great treasure buried in a field. No one is sure how he discovered it.

Maybe he was walking by a lake when a bottle washed ashore — and inside the bottle was a map!

Maybe he was resting under a tree when he saw something glimmer in the sunlight. He picked it up, dusted it off, and saw that it was a brilliant sapphire. Looking around, he saw that all around him were scattered hundreds of jewels, lying in the dust.

Or maybe he struck the wooden top of a treasure chest while he was digging potatoes.

It doesn't really matter how it happened. All we need to know is that he found a great treasure. We can imagine a chest overflowing with diamonds, rubies, gold and silver coins, emerald rings, strings of pearls, and jeweled goblets. He was quite excited.

There was only one problem: The field where he found the treasure didn't belong to him. It was someone else's property.

So what did he do? He rushed home and gathered everything he owned — and he sold it all, everything he had. Then he ran to his relatives and friends asking them to lend him all the money they could spare. He wanted to do everything he could to buy that field where the treasure lay. He wanted to get there first with the money. He just couldn't believe that such adventure could happen to such an ordinary man. These things, he thought, only happen in fairy tales.

He collected a huge sum of money and went off to find the owner of the field. The owner thought the man was crazy, out of his mind. It's just a useless old field. It's not worth the trouble it would take to trim the weeds.

But the young man knew better. The two

shook hands on the deal. And our hero became the wealthiest person in the land.

These things don't only happen in storybooks. That story, in fact, is one that Jesus told to His disciples. You'll find it in the Bible, in a shorter form. Jesus told that story because He wanted to help us understand something very important.

Jesus wanted you and me to know that there is a great treasure waiting for us, too. The treasure is Jesus' teaching and His love, and it can make us happier than all the money in the world.

We can gain this treasure for ourselves whenever we say yes to Jesus. Not just in big things, like being a hero and saving someone's life. We store up great treasures for ourselves whenever we make the smallest acts of faith, whenever we hear the Word of God and hold it close to our hearts.

Every time we accept what Jesus and His Church teach us, we are plunking down a couple of coins and buying a King's chamber full of jewels.

How hard are we willing to work, as the young man in the story did, to obtain God's treasure?

In the pages of this book, you'll find many short questions and answers, each explaining one of the saving truths that Jesus taught us, and all based on the *Catechism of the Catholic Church*. Each time you come to know and accept one of these little sayings; each time you make an effort to put it into practice by living as Jesus taught us; each time you love God with your whole heart; each time you love your neighbor — then you are buying a field that Jesus Himself planted with riches.

That field is the Catholic Church, and all its riches are yours for the taking: its teachings, its sacraments, and its gifts of the Holy

Spirit. Jesus made His Church good and true, and He made it to last forever. He gave it all that it would need to make people happy right here on earth — by knowing God and loving Him and serving Him. Jesus also made His Church to be the one sure road to heaven for all God's children.

Finally, Jesus gave Himself to the Church in a very special way. In the sacraments, especially the Eucharist, He comes to everyone who will welcome Him — and He becomes one with that person. Imagine: God, Who made the stars and volcanoes, dinosaurs and comets, wants to be that close in friendship with us.

This is the truth of the Catholic Faith, and it's the treasure you will find in the pages of this book. So read on, and take each treasure as your own, one at a time.

— *The Authors*

NOTE: With each question and answer, and with each prayer in "A Treasury of Prayers," there is a notation advising what grade levels are appropriate for that particular teaching. For example, **(Pre-8)** indicates that the material is appropriate for preschool through grade eight. These levels were determined using standard catechetical guidelines.

PART ONE
Believing the Faith

1. Who are you?
My name is _____. I am a child of God, created in His image and likeness. **(Pre-8)**

2. Who is God?
God is Love. Out of love, He made the world and everything in it. Out of love, He made me and watches over me constantly. **(Pre-8)**

3. Why did God make you?
God made me to know Him, to love Him, and to serve Him here on earth, so that I may live with Him forever in heaven. **(K-8)**

4. What is the Holy Trinity?
The Holy Trinity is the mystery of God. God is a Trinity because He is three Persons — Father, Son, and Holy Spirit — yet one God. **(2-8)**

5. Who is God the Father?
God the Father is the first Person of the Holy Trinity. He is a true and perfect Father, Who guards us, His children, guides us, is always attentive to us, and provides for our needs. **(Pre-8)**

6. Who is Jesus?
Jesus is the eternal Son of God, the second Person of the Holy Trinity, Who came into the world to save us from sin and show us the

way to heaven. Jesus is true God and true man. **(Pre-8)**

7. *How was Jesus born into this world?*
By the power of the Holy Spirit, Jesus became man and was born to the Virgin Mary. When God became man, He became our brother. **(1-8)**

8. *How did Jesus live?*
Jesus worked, studied, and prayed as we all must do. He lived with His parents, Mary and Joseph, as an obedient and loving son. **(Pre-8)**

9. *What are miracles?*
Miracles are acts of God. They show that God's power is greater than every other power, even the power of nature. **(1-8)**

10. *Did Jesus perform miracles?*
Jesus performed many miracles. He changed

water into wine, He healed the sick, He brought the dead to life, and He fed thousands of people with a few loaves of bread. **(1-8)**

11. *How did Jesus die?*

Jesus died on the cross. People who did not believe in Jesus put Him to death. But Jesus still loved them. He said, "Forgive them, Father, for they do not know what they are doing" (Luke 23:34). **(1-8)**

12. *Why did Jesus die on the cross?*

Jesus died on the cross for my sake. He died to make up for all my sins and to open the gates of heaven for all of God's people. **(1-8)**

13. *What happened after Jesus died?*

His mother and His friends laid Him in a tomb. After three days, Jesus rose from the dead. We call this "the Resurrection." We celebrate the Resurrection on every Sunday, but especially Easter Sunday. **(1-8)**

14. What is the Ascension?

Forty days after rising from the dead, Jesus ascended to heaven, where He sits at the right hand of God the Father forever. **(4-8)**

15. Who is the Holy Spirit?

The Holy Spirit is the third Person of the Holy Trinity. Jesus sent the Holy Spirit to His apostles on Pentecost, ten days after Jesus' ascension. He continues to fill believers with His Spirit today. **(1-8)**

16. What does the Holy Spirit do?

The Holy Spirit gives us the power to be faithful to God and to do all that God asks of us. The Holy Spirit comes to us at baptism and at confirmation. **(1-8)**

17. Who were the apostles?

The apostles were twelve men Jesus called to be His special friends and leaders in His Church. As witnesses to the Resurrection, they were sent by Jesus to every corner of the world to tell His good news. **(3-8)**

18. Who was St. Peter?
St. Peter was the man Jesus chose to lead His Church. St. Peter was the first pope. **(3-8)**

19. What is a pope?
Following after St. Peter, the pope is the supreme head of the Church on earth. **(3-8)**

20. Who are the bishops?
The bishops are successors to the apostles. They teach, guide, and sanctify the people of God throughout the world. **(3-8)**

21. What is the Church?
The Church is the Living Body of Jesus today. It is made up of all God's people. Jesus made the Church to be the ordinary way people could come to know God and be saved. **(1-8)**

22. Why do we go to church?

We go to church to receive God's grace, especially in His Body and Blood in Holy Communion. We go to church to gather with the people of God, to thank God for His gifts, and to take part in — to remember and give thanks for — the great sacrifice of Jesus on the cross, which is made present in the Mass. **(1-8)**

23. Who is the Blessed Virgin Mary?

The Blessed Virgin Mary is the mother of Jesus. Because Jesus is God the Son, we call her the "Mother of God." She is Mother of the Church and our mother, too. **(1-8)**

24. Why is Mary important?

Mary is the model disciple, who gave God perfect obedience, always saying yes to Him. She was chosen, from all time, to bear God into the world. **(1-8)**

25. What is the Rosary?

The Rosary is a series of prayers, counted on beads, which we offer to Mary as we think about the life of Jesus. **(3-8)**

26. What is a saint?

The saints are Christians who have died and joined God in heaven. We honor them because they lived holy lives. **(2-8)**

27. Why do we pray to saints?

Our Faith tells us that in heaven the saints pray for us on earth. Just as we might ask our best friend on earth to pray for us, we ask these good friends in heaven to pray for us. **(2-8)**

28. What happens when someone dies?

People who follow the will of God go to Him at the end of their days on earth. His mercy purifies them of their sins so that they can live in His presence. **(2-8)**

29. What is heaven?

Heaven is life with God in His kingdom forever. It is a state of total joy and peace, where there is no suffering. **(3-8)**

30. What is purgatory?

Purgatory is the purification a soul goes through after death so that it can enter heaven. **(5-8)**

31. What is hell?

Hell is a state of eternal punishment for people who die in serious sin, choosing not to love God or follow His commandments. **(5-8)**

32. What are angels?

Angels are pure spirits without bodies. They serve as God's special messengers and helpers. The Bible mentions three archangels by name: Gabriel, Raphael, and Michael. **(2-8)**

33. *What are guardian angels?*

Guardian angels watch over us, helping us to do good and avoid evil. God gives everyone a guardian angel. **(2-8)**

PART TWO
Celebrating the Faith

34. What is a sacrament?
A sacrament is an outward sign instituted by Jesus to give grace. Through the sacraments, Jesus touches and blesses our lives. **(2-8)**

35. What is grace?
Grace is our sharing in the life of God. **(2-8)**

36. How do we receive God's grace?
God gives us grace as a free gift. Grace comes to us in many ways through the Holy Spirit,

but most especially we receive this grace in the Church and her sacraments. **(2-8)**

37. How many sacraments are there?
There are seven sacraments. They are baptism, confirmation, the Eucharist, penance, marriage (or "matrimony"), holy orders, and the anointing of the sick. **(3-8)**

38. Where do the sacraments get their power to give grace?
The power comes from Jesus' own life, especially His suffering, death, and resurrection. God's power works through the sacraments in spite of our own weakness. **(3-8)**

39. Do we always receive grace in the sacraments?
The sacraments always give grace. But we have to be ready to receive that grace. We need to prepare our hearts so that we are in a state of grace. **(3-8)**

40. What is the state of grace?
Living as God wishes us to live, free from mortal sin. **(3-8)**

41. Are the sacraments necessary for salvation?
Yes. Jesus made the sacraments as the ordinary way to salvation. In His mercy, God gives His graces in extraordinary ways, but the sacraments remain the normal way people are saved. **(3-8)**

42. Where are the sacraments found?
The sacraments are celebrated within the Church Jesus founded, the Catholic Church. **(3-8)**

43. Who ordinarily administers the sacraments?
The ordinary minister of the sacraments is a bishop or a priest, who acts in the person of Jesus Christ. **(3-8)**

44. How often can we receive the sacraments?

Some sacraments can be received only once because they leave a permanent spiritual mark on the Christian's soul. They are baptism, confirmation, and holy orders. Other sacraments should be received frequently, especially penance and the Eucharist. **(3-8)**

45. How are the sacraments divided?

They are the sacraments of initiation (baptism, confirmation, and the Eucharist); the sacraments of healing (penance and the anointing of the sick); and the sacraments at the service of communion — in other words, sacraments directed toward the salvation of others (marriage and holy orders). **(5-8)**

46. What is baptism?

Baptism is the sacrament that takes away original sin and makes us sons and daughters of

God. By baptism, we become members of the Church. **(1-8)**

47. *What is original sin?*

It is the sin of the first humans, our first parents, who disobeyed God. All people share in the effects and the guilt of that sin: suffering, illness, death, and the tendency to sin. The guilt of original sin can only be removed by baptism. **(4-8)**

48. *How is baptism celebrated?*

While pouring water over the head of the person, the minister of baptism says, "I baptize you in the name of the Father, and of the Son, and of the Holy Spirit." The person is then anointed with holy chrism. The baptized person receives a white garment and a candle, meaning that he or she is now a child of God, enlightened by Jesus. **(1-8)**

49. Who can receive baptism?

Anyone, at any age, can be baptized. Adults enter the Church through the Rite of Christian Initiation of Adults. Infants should receive baptism as soon as possible after their birth. **(4-8)**

50. Why does the Church baptize babies?

Jesus said, "Let the little children come to Me, and do not hinder them" (Matthew 19:14; also see Mark 10:14 and Luke 18:16). Every person is in need of God's grace. Every baby born should be set free from original sin and enabled to live as God wants us to live. **(4-8)**

51. What is confirmation?

Confirmation is the sacrament through which we receive the gifts and the fruits of the Holy Spirit, strengthening us to be witnesses of Jesus Christ. **(4-8)**

52. What are the gifts of the Holy Spirit?
There are seven gifts of the Holy Spirit: wisdom, understanding, counsel, fortitude, knowledge, piety, and fear of the Lord. **(5-8)**

53. What are the fruits of the Holy Spirit?
The fruits of the Holy Spirit are charity, joy, peace, patience, kindness, goodness, generosity, gentleness, faithfulness, modesty, self-control, and chastity. **(7-8)**

54. Who can receive confirmation?
Every baptized person should receive the sacrament of confirmation. **(6-8)**

55. What does confirmation do?
By the power of the Holy Spirit, confirmation unites us more closely with Jesus and the Church, giving us enlightenment and courage to share and to defend the Faith. **(5-8)**

56. Who administers confirmation?
Usually, the bishop administers confirmation. **(5-8)**

57. How does the bishop give confirmation?
The bishop extends his hands over each person to be confirmed, anoints the forehead with holy chrism, and prays, "Be sealed with the gift of the Holy Spirit." **(6-8)**

58. What is the Eucharist?
The Eucharist is the sacrament that contains the Body, Blood, Soul, and Divinity of Jesus Christ under the form (or "species") of bread and wine. **(2-8)**

59. When did Jesus give us the Eucharist?
Jesus gave us the Eucharist on Holy Thursday, at the Last Supper. **(2-8)**

60. How did Jesus give us the Eucharist?
Jesus blessed the bread, broke it, and gave it to His apostles, saying, "Take this, all of you, and eat it: this is My Body." He took the cup of wine, blessed it, and gave it to them, saying, "Take this, all of you, and drink from it: this is the cup of My Blood" (see Matthew 26:26-28; Mark 14:22-24; Luke 22:19-20). **(2-8)**

61. How does Jesus' action continue today?
The sacrament of the Eucharist takes place in the Mass when the priest consecrates the bread and wine and prays the blessing of Jesus. **(2-8)**

62. What is the Mass?
The Mass is the sacrifice of Jesus on the cross, extended through time and space. Through the Mass, the sacrifice offered once and for all on the cross is made ever present. **(2-8)**

63. What happens to the bread and wine?
When the priest consecrates these gifts, the bread and wine become the Body and Blood of Jesus. We call this the "Real Presence." The change that takes place is called "transubstantiation." **(2-8)**

64. How long is Jesus present in the sacrament?
Jesus remains present in the Eucharist, even after the Mass, when the sacrament is ordinarily kept in a special place called the "tabernacle." **(2-8)**

65. Why did Jesus give us the sacrament of the Eucharist?
He gave us the sacrament so that we could be deeply united with Him and His Church, to increase His grace within us, and to strengthen us in our struggle against sin. **(2-8)**

66. How do we receive the Holy Eucharist?

We receive the Body and Blood of Jesus at Holy Communion, normally during the Mass. **(2-8)**

67. How should we prepare to receive Holy Communion?

We should keep Jesus in mind, and we should speak to Him in prayer. Above all, we should be in the state of grace. The best way to stay in the state of grace is by going regularly to the sacrament of penance. Also, we must fast for an hour before receiving Holy Communion. **(2-8)**

68. What is required by the Communion fast?

We must go without food or drink for one hour. Water or medicine never breaks the fast. **(2-8)**

69. Who celebrates the sacrament of the Eucharist?
Only an ordained priest can consecrate the bread and wine so that they become the Body and Blood of Jesus. **(2-8)**

70. How often may we receive Holy Communion?
We should receive Holy Communion as often as we can, even every day. We may receive Holy Communion no more than twice in a single day. **(2-8)**

71. Why is the Eucharist so important?
The Eucharist is the fullness of our sharing in the life of Jesus. It sums up our entire Faith. It is the source of God's grace for the Christian today. It is the presence of God among us. **(2-8)**

72. What is the sacrament of penance?
It is the sacrament through which God

forgives our sins and reconciles us with Himself and His Church. **(2-8)**

73. *What are other names for the sacrament of penance?*
The sacrament of penance is also called "the sacrament of reconciliation," "the sacrament of forgiveness," "the sacrament of confession," and "the sacrament of conversion." **(2-8)**

74. *When did Jesus give us the sacrament of penance?*
Jesus gave the authority to forgive sins to the apostles when He said, "I will give you the keys of the kingdom of heaven, and whatever you bind on earth will be bound in heaven, and whatever you loose on earth will be loosed in heaven" (Matthew 16:19). This power continues today through the ministry of the bishops and priests, who follow in the footsteps of the apostles. **(2-8)**

75. How do priests give us God's forgiveness?

They forgive sins, in the name of Jesus Christ, through the prayer of absolution. **(2-8)**

76. Why do we need the sacrament of penance?

Because all of us sin, and the Bible says that even the best people sin every day. Our sins are offenses against God, and only God can forgive sins. **(2-8)**

77. What makes a good confession?

Penance requires that we be sorry for our sins, that we confess them to a priest, and that we complete the penance assigned to us by the priest. **(2-8)**

78. How often should we go to confession?

If we have committed a mortal sin, we should go immediately. But we should also make a habit of frequent confession of ordinary (venial) sins. **(3-8)**

79. Why should we go to penance so often?
Frequent confession of venial sins helps us to form our conscience, to overcome habits of sin, and to grow in holiness. **(3-8)**

80. How should we prepare for confession?
The best way to prepare for confession is by making a daily examination of conscience. **(2-8)**

81. What is an examination of conscience?
The examination of conscience is a prayerful look at our actions, thoughts, and words, to determine how faithful we have been to the commandments of God. **(2-8)**

82. What is the sacrament of the anointing of the sick?
It is the sacrament that brings healing, comfort, and strength, through the grace of the Holy Spirit, to those who are sick or elderly. **(4-8)**

83. Why should the sick be anointed?
Jesus showed constant care for sick people. In the Bible, we read that St. James the Apostle wrote to the early Church: "Is anyone among you sick? Let him call for the priests and let them pray over him, anointing him with oil" (James 5:14). **(4-8)**

84. How is the sacrament of the anointing of the sick celebrated?
An ordained priest lays his hands on the sick person, prays, and anoints the person with oil. **(4-8)**

85. Who should receive the anointing of the sick?

Ordinarily, the sacrament is received by people who are seriously ill, in danger of death, or very old. **(4-8)**

86. What does the sick person receive in the sacrament of the anointing of the sick?

The sick person receives grace to be strong in facing illness. The sick person receives the forgiveness of sins. Sometimes, the person also receives healing of the illness. **(4-8)**

87. What is the sacrament of holy orders?

Holy orders is the sacrament by which bishops, priests, and deacons are ordained to carry on the mission of Jesus and His apostles. **(4-8)**

88. When did Jesus establish holy orders?

Jesus established the priesthood of His new covenant at the Last Supper, on Holy Thursday, when He instituted the Eucharist and told His apostles, "Do this in memory of Me" (Luke 22:19; also see 1 Corinthians 11:24-25). **(4-8)**

89. Who can receive holy orders?
The Church gives the sacrament of holy orders to baptized men who have been called by God and who have been judged ready for ministry to the Church. **(4-8)**

90. How is the sacrament administered?
The bishop administers the sacrament by laying his hands on the man and praying over him. **(5-8)**

91. How is a man changed by holy orders?
Ordination gives a man an indelible spiritual mark. This mark is permanent. Once ordained, a man is a priest forever. In celebrating the sacraments, a priest acts in the person of Jesus Christ. **(6-8)**

92. What are the primary works of the priest?

Priests are ordained to serve the people of God, by teaching them, guiding them, and sanctifying them. **(4-8)**

93. What is the sacrament of marriage?

Marriage is the sacrament that brings together a man and a woman in a holy and lifelong bond so that, as a couple, they can grow closer to each other and to God, and bring children into the world. **(5-8)**

94. Who can receive the sacrament of marriage?

A baptized man and a baptized woman who are prepared and are free to make such a commitment can receive this sacrament. **(5-8)**

95. Who are the ministers of the sacrament?

The ministers of marriage are the man and the woman. **(5-8)**

96. When does the sacrament take place?
The sacrament takes place, in the Church, when the man and the woman freely exchange their consent to be married. The priest receives their consent and gives the blessing of the Church. **(5-8)**

97. What is required of the man and the woman who are married?
They must love each other totally, for the rest of their lives, and be open to children as a gift from God. **(5-8)**

98. What is a sacramental?
A sacramental is any action or thing blessed by the Church to inspire Christians to prayer and love of God. These include the Sign of the Cross, holy water, prayers of blessing, works of art, rosaries, candles, blessed ashes, blessed palms, medals, and scapulars. **(5-8)**

99. What do sacramentals do?

They prepare the heart and mind to be more open to grace. They do not convey God's grace as sacraments do. **(5-8)**

PART THREE
Living the Faith

100. What must we do to gain God's promise of salvation and happiness?
We must follow the way of Christ by loving God and neighbor and following the commandments. This is called "the moral life." **(5-8)**

101. How did Jesus sum up this moral life?
Jesus said that the greatest commandment is to love God with all your heart, soul, and

mind, and to love your neighbor as yourself. **(6-8)**

102. What are the commandments of God?
On Mount Sinai, God gave Moses the Ten
Commandments:

1. I am the Lord your God: you shall
   not have strange Gods before Me.
2. You shall not take the name of the
   Lord your God in vain.
3. Remember to keep holy the Lord's
   Day.
4. Honor your father and your mother.
5. You shall not kill.
6. You shall not commit adultery.
7. You shall not steal.
8. You shall not bear false witness
   against your neighbor.
9. You shall not covet your neighbor's
   wife.
10. You shall not covet your neighbor's
    goods.

(A traditional catechetical formula, from the *Catechism of the Catholic Church*.) **(4-8)**

103. What does the first commandment require?
The first commandment teaches us to love God with all our heart, mind, and soul. This commandment requires our total loyalty to the one true Faith and forbids us to make anything else more important than God in our lives. **(4-8)**

104. How do we give honor to God?
We honor God by praying to Him, offering Him fitting worship, and keeping to the way of life He gave us. **(1-8)**

105. How can the first commandment be broken?
The first commandment can be broken by turning away from the Catholic Faith, by putting other things before God in our lives, or

by believing in superstition, magic, or false religion. **(2-8)**

106. What does the second commandment require?
We must honor the name of God by speaking of Him reverently and not using His name in a disrespectful way. **(4-8)**

107. How can the second commandment be broken?
We can abuse God's name by speaking badly of Him, by failing to show respect for His name, by referring to Him with hatred or defiance, and by using His name to curse people. This commandment also forbids us to swear falsely by God's name. **(2-8)**

108. What does the third commandment teach?
The third commandment calls us to keep holy the Lord's Day, Sunday. **(4-8)**

109. How do we keep Sunday holy?
We keep Sunday holy, first of all, by going to Mass, which we are required to do by our Catholic Faith. **(1-8)**

110. How else do we keep Sunday holy?
We keep the day holy by resting from work, doing good deeds, and spending time reading the Bible and praying. **(1-8)**

111. What does the third commandment forbid?
The third commandment forbids us to do work that is unnecessary and keeps our minds and hearts from the worship owed to God. We should also avoid making others do such work. **(2-8)**

112. What else does the third commandment require?
The third commandment requires us to attend Mass on holy days of obligation, and to treat

those special days as we would treat a Sunday. **(3-8)**

113. What does the fourth commandment teach?
The fourth commandment tells us to honor our parents. **(4-8)**

114. How do we honor our parents?
We honor our parents by loving, respecting, and obeying them, and by helping them to keep a bright and cheerful home and to build a strong family. **(1-8)**

115. Why do we work to build a strong family?
The family is the building block of society, and every home is a church, a holy place that reflects the love of God. **(3-8)**

116. Does the requirement extend beyond honor for our parents?

Yes, the fourth commandment requires that we give obedience to all rightful authority in family, Church, and state. **(6-8)**

117. What are the sins against the fourth commandment?

People break the fourth commandment by being selfish and unforgiving toward family members, irresponsible in fulfilling their duties at home, and disobedient or disrespectful to their elders. **(2-8)**

118. What does the fifth commandment teach?

The fifth commandment teaches us not to kill. **(4-8)**

119. Why does God command us not to kill?

God commands us not to kill because

human life is sacred, from its beginning to its end. Human life is made in God's image. No one, under any circumstances, may destroy an innocent human life. **(6-8)**

120. How can we best fulfill the fifth commandment?
We fulfill the fifth commandment by living in peace with all our neighbors, by respecting their rights, and by taking proper care of ourselves and others. **(1-8)**

121. What is forbidden by the fifth commandment?
Murder, abortion, euthanasia, suicide, and abuse of our bodies are the gravest offenses against the fifth commandment. **(2-8)**

122. Does the fifth commandment forbid anything else?
Jesus said that the commandment also forbids anger, revenge, hatred, and fighting. **(2-8)**

123. What does the sixth commandment teach?

The sixth commandment teaches that people should not commit adultery. **(4-8)**

124. What does the sixth commandment require?

The sixth commandment requires us to be pure, chaste, and modest, and to be faithful to the vocation God has given us. **(5-8)**

125. What is chastity?

Chastity is the virtue that enables us to take charge of our body's passions and desires and keep them in line with God's will. To be chaste, one must pray. **(5-8)**

126. What is modesty?

Modesty means respecting the privacy of intimate details of everyone's life. This is shown by the way we talk, dress, act, and even the way we look at one another. **(5-8)**

127. What are the sins against the sixth commandment?

The sixth commandment forbids any actions outside of marriage that belong only in marriage, such as the signs of affection between a husband and wife. The sixth commandment forbids us to violate another person's privacy by our looks or actions. The sixth commandment also forbids us to view immodest or indecent books, movies, or television programs. **(2-8)**

128. What does the seventh commandment teach?

The seventh commandment teaches us not to steal. **(4-8)**

129. What does the seventh commandment require?

The seventh commandment asks us to live in charity with our neighbors, showing respect for the people and the goods of the earth and sharing them justly. **(1-8)**

130. Does the seventh commandment require anything more?
Jesus said we have a special duty to care for the poor through acts of kindness and mercy. **(6-8)**

131. How are we to live in charity with our neighbors?
The seventh commandment calls us to respect their property and pay whatever we owe them. **(1-8)**

132. What does the seventh commandment forbid?
The seventh commandment forbids stealing, withholding money or things that rightly belong to someone else, and selfishly refusing to share our goods. **(2-8)**

*133. What does the eighth command-
ment teach?*

The eighth commandment teaches us to tell
the truth at all times. **(4-8)**

*134. What does the eighth command-
ment forbid?*

The eighth commandment forbids us to tell
lies, spread gossip, ruin another's reputation,
exaggerate, boast, or hold back information
that should be told. **(2-8)**

*135. What does the ninth commandment
teach?*

The ninth commandment teaches us to keep
our thoughts pure. **(4-8)**

*136. What does the ninth commandment
forbid?*

The ninth commandment forbids unchaste
thoughts and desires that go against faithfulness to one's vocation. **(2-8)**

137. How do we remain pure in our thoughts?

Purity of heart requires modesty in dress and speech. Purity comes from living a chaste and prayerful life. **(5-8)**

138. What does the tenth commandment teach?

The tenth commandment teaches us to be satisfied with what we have and to be grateful to God. **(4-8)**

139. What does the tenth commandment forbid?

The tenth commandment forbids us to be jealous of others or their possessions. **(2-8)**

140. What are the sins against the tenth commandment?

The sins against the tenth commandment are greed and envy. **(2-8)**

141. Why should Christians obey the commandments of God?

So that they can live in freedom and gain the salvation that Christ won for everyone. **(4-8)**

142. What are the precepts of the Church?

The precepts of the Church are the duties of every Catholic. They are:

1. Go to Mass on Sundays and holy days of obligation.
2. Receive Holy Communion and confession regularly.
3. Study Catholic teaching.
4. Observe the marriage laws of the Church.
5. Support the Church financially.
6. Observe the prescribed days for fasting and abstinence.
7. Join in the missionary work of the Church. **(4-8)**

143. How do we live in freedom?
We are truly free when we choose to do what is right, what God wants us to do. We lose our freedom when we choose to break the commandments and do evil. **(2-8)**

144. How do we protect our freedom?
We protect our freedom by forming the conscience that God gave us. A well-formed conscience is God's voice speaking in our hearts, helping us to do good. **(2-8)**

145. How do we form our conscience?
We form our conscience by praying, reading the Scriptures, receiving the sacraments, following the advice of our parents and priests, and knowing the teachings of the Church. **(2-8)**

146. What is the surest way we can continue on the way of Christ, even when it is difficult?

The surest way we can continue on the way of Christ is by forming good habits of mind, heart, and action. These habits are called "virtues." **(6-8)**

147. What are the most important virtues?

The most important virtues are those given to us by God, called the "theological virtues." They are faith, hope, and charity. **(6-8)**

148. What are the most important human virtues?

The most important human virtues are prudence (or sound judgment), justice, fortitude (bravery and strength), and temperance (self-control). **(6-8)**

149. What are the works of mercy?
The works of mercy are charitable deeds by which we help our neighbor. They are usually divided into "corporal" and "spiritual" works. **(6-8)**

150. What are the corporal works of mercy?
The corporal (physical) works of mercy are feeding the hungry, sheltering the homeless, clothing the naked, visiting the sick, and burying the dead. **(6-8)**

151. What are the spiritual works of mercy?
The spiritual works of mercy are instructing the ignorant, advising the doubtful, correcting the sinner, comforting the afflicted, forgiving wrongs, bearing wrongs patiently, and praying for the living and the dead. **(6-8)**

PART FOUR
Praying the Faith

152. What is prayer?
Prayer is raising one's heart and mind to God, and asking good things of God. Prayer is talking with God. **(Pre-8)**

153. When should we pray?
The Bible says we should pray always, meaning that we should be aware of God's presence at all times. But we also need to set special times when we can be alone with God. **(K-8)**

154. What are the best times for special prayer?

It is important that we set time aside for prayer at the beginning and end of each day. Sundays and holy days are times the Church marks especially for prayer. **(Pre-8)**

155. What makes good prayer?

When we pray well, we are attentive to God, we trust in Him and His grace, and we continue even when we find prayer difficult. **(5-8)**

156. Who helps us to pray?

Jesus gave us the Holy Spirit to help us in our prayer. The Holy Spirit also works through the Church to help us pray. **(2-8)**

157. What are the different kinds of prayer?

There are four main kinds of prayer: adoration, which honors God for His goodness and majesty; petition, which asks things of

God; intercession, which we offer for the good of other people; contrition, which shows our sorrow for our sins; and thanksgiving, which shows our gratitude. **(2-8)**

158. How did Jesus say we should pray?
Jesus gave us a model for prayer by His life of prayer. He gave us a perfect prayer in the Our Father. **(2-8)**

159. Why is the Our Father the perfect prayer?
The Our Father sums up the whole Gospel. It tells of our dependence on God, our trust in His goodness, and our desire to do His will and live with Him forever. **(6-8)**

160. What other prayers does the Church recommend?
The Sign of the Cross, the Hail Mary, the Glory Be, the Apostles' Creed, the Acts of Faith, Hope, and Love, the Act of Contrition, and

the Rosary are the most commonly used prayers in the Church. There are many others that can help us to pray well. **(6-8)**

PRACTICING
YOUR FAITH

A TREASURY
OF PRAYERS

The Sign of the Cross

In the name of the Father, and of the Son,
and of the Holy Spirit. Amen. **(Pre-8)**

The Our Father

Our Father, Who art in heaven,
hallowed be Thy name.
Thy kingdom come.
Thy will be done on earth as it is in heaven.
Give us this day our daily bread.
And forgive us our trespasses
as we forgive those who trespass against us.
And lead us not into temptation,
but deliver us from evil. Amen. **(K-8)**

The Hail Mary

Hail Mary, full of grace,
the Lord is with thee.
Blessed art thou among women,
and blessed is the fruit of thy womb, Jesus.
Holy Mary, Mother of God,
pray for us sinners
now and at the hour of our death. Amen.
(1-8)

The Glory Be

Glory be to the Father,
and to the Son,
and to the Holy Spirit.
As it was in the beginning,
is now, and ever shall be,
world without end. Amen. **(1-8)**

The Apostles' Creed

I believe in God, the Father almighty,
Creator of heaven and earth;

and in Jesus Christ, His only Son, our Lord,
Who was conceived by the Holy Spirit,
born of the Virgin Mary,
suffered under Pontius Pilate,
was crucified, died, and was buried.
He descended into hell;
the third day He rose again from the dead.
He ascended into heaven
and sits at the right hand of God, the Father
almighty.
From thence He shall come to judge the
living and the dead.
I believe in the Holy Spirit,
the holy Catholic Church,
the communion of saints,
the forgiveness of sins,
the resurrection of the body,
and life everlasting. Amen. **(2-8)**

Act of Contrition

O my God, I am heartily sorry
for having offended You,

and I detest all my sins
because of Your just punishments,
but most of all because they offend You,
   my God,
Who are all good and deserving of all my
   love.
I firmly resolve, with the help of Your grace,
to sin no more and to avoid the near
   occasions of sin. Amen. **(2-8)**

Grace at Meals

Before the meal:
Bless us, O Lord, and these Your gifts, which
we are about to receive from Your bounty,
through Christ our Lord. Amen. **(Pre-8)**

After the meal:
We give You thanks, almighty God, for these
and all Your gifts, which we have received
from Your bounty through Christ our Lord.
Amen. **(1-8)**

Hail Holy Queen

Hail Holy Queen, mother of mercy,
our life, our sweetness, and our hope,
to you do we cry, poor banished children of
Eve;
to you do we send up our sighs,
mourning and weeping in this valley of tears.
Turn, then, O most gracious advocate,
your eyes of mercy toward us,
and after this our exile
show to us the blessed fruit of your womb,
Jesus.
O clement, O loving, O sweet Virgin Mary.
Pray for us, O holy Mother of God,
that we may be made worthy of the
promises of Christ. **(3-8)**

The Rosary

1. Begin with the Sign of the Cross.
2. Holding the cross at the end of the beads,
   pray the Apostles' Creed.

3. On the first bead, pray the Our Father.
4. On each of the next three beads, pray a Hail Mary. Then pray a Glory Be.
5. The rest of the beads follow a pattern: one bead by itself, followed by ten beads together. On the bead by itself, pray an Our Father. On each of the ten beads, pray a Hail Mary.
6. Each set of ten beads is called a "decade." On each decade, we remember one of the events in the lives of Jesus and Mary. Try to picture that event, and talk to Jesus about it in your heart.
7. End each decade with a Glory Be.
8. At the end of all the beads, pray the Hail Holy Queen. **(3-8)**

The Mysteries of the Rosary

The Joyful Mysteries
(prayed Mondays and Thursdays)

1. The Annunciation
2. The Visitation

3. The Birth of Jesus
4. The Presentation of Jesus in the Temple
5. The Finding of Jesus in the Temple

The Sorrowful Mysteries
(prayed Tuesdays and Fridays)

1. The Agony in the Garden
2. The Scourging at the Pillar
3. The Crowning with Thorns
4. The Carrying of the Cross
5. The Crucifixion and Death

The Glorious Mysteries
(prayed Wednesdays, Saturdays,
and Sundays)

1. The Resurrection
2. The Ascension
3. The Descent of the Holy Spirit upon the Apostles
4. The Assumption of Mary into Heaven
5. The Crowning of Mary in Heaven **(3-8)**

Act of Faith

O my God, I firmly believe that You are one God in three divine Persons: Father, Son, and Holy Spirit. I believe that Your divine Son became man and died for our sins, and that He will come to judge the living and the dead. I believe these and all the truths which the holy Catholic Church teaches, because You have revealed them, Who can neither deceive nor be deceived. In this Faith I desire to live and die. Amen. **(7, 8)**

Act of Hope

O my God, trusting in Your promises and the infinite merits of Jesus Christ, our Redeemer, I hope for the pardon of my sins and the graces I need to serve You faithfully on earth, and to obtain eternal life in heaven. Amen. **(7, 8)**

Act of Love

O my God, I love You above all things, with my whole heart and soul, because You are infinitely good and deserving of all my love. I love my neighbor as myself for love of You. Amen. **(7, 8)**

Prayer to the Holy Spirit

Come, Holy Spirit, fill the hearts of Your faithful and enkindle in them the fire of Your divine love. Send forth Your Spirit and they shall be created, and You shall renew the face of the earth. O God, Who instructs the hearts of the faithful by the light of the Holy Spirit, grant us by the same Spirit to be truly wise and ever to rejoice in His consolations. Amen. **(5-8)**

Simple Prayers

Jesus, I love You.
Thank You, God.
God, how great You are. **(Pre-8)**

Prayer for the Dead

Eternal rest grant to them, O Lord, and let perpetual light shine upon them. May they rest in peace. Amen. **(5-8)**

A Morning Prayer

God our Father, I offer You today all that I think and do and say. I offer it with what was done on earth by Jesus Christ, Your Son. **(4-8)**

Prayer at Midday
(The Angelus)

The angel of the Lord declared unto Mary.
And she conceived by the Holy Spirit.
Hail Mary, full of grace . . .
Behold the handmaid of the Lord.
Let it be done to me according to your word.
Hail Mary, full of grace . . .
And the Word was made flesh.
And dwelt among us.
Hail Mary, full of grace . . .

Pray for us, O holy Mother of God.
That we may be made worthy of the
    promises of Christ.
Let us pray. Pour forth, we beseech You, O
Lord, Your grace into our hearts, that we to
whom the Incarnation of Christ, Your Son,
was made known by the message of an angel, may by His Passion and cross be brought
to the glory of His resurrection, through the
same Christ our Lord. Amen. **(7, 8)**

Easter Season Prayer at Midday
(The Regina Caeli)

O Queen of heaven, rejoice! Alleluia!
For He Whom you merited to bear! Alleluia!
Has risen as He said! Alleluia!
Pray for us to God! Alleluia!
Rejoice and be glad, O Virgin Mary!
    Alleluia!
For the Lord has risen indeed! Alleluia!
O God, Who through the resurrection of Your
Son, our Lord Jesus Christ, willed to fill the

world with joy, grant, we beseech You, that through His Virgin Mother, Mary, we may come to the joys of everlasting life, through the same Christ our Lord. Amen. **(7, 8)**

Holy Days of Obligation in the United States

Mary, Mother of God, January 1
The Ascension, 40 days after Easter
The Assumption of the Blessed Virgin Mary,
    August 15
All Saints, November 1
The Immaculate Conception, December 8
Christmas Day, December 25 **(7, 8)**

HOW TO PRAY
THE MASS

Prayer doesn't get any better than the Mass.

Since the earliest days of the Church, the Mass has been the high point of Christian prayer, and the source of Christians' strength and courage.

Jesus wanted it to be that way. At the Last Supper, He took bread and broke it, saying, "This is My Body." Then He took a cup of wine and blessed it, calling it the "blood of the covenant" (Matthew 26:26-28). He then commanded His apostles: "Do this in memory of Me" (Luke 22:19; also see 1 Corinthians 11:24-25).

Elsewhere, He told His friends about His presence in the Eucharist. He said that the Eucharist was necessary for Christian life: "I am the living bread which came down from heaven; if anyone eats of this bread, he will live forever" (John 6:51).

In the Eucharist, which we celebrate in the Mass, Jesus is made *really present*, though the bread and wine continue to look and taste and feel like ordinary bread and wine. After the priest says Jesus' words of consecration — "This is My Body. . . . This is the cup of My Blood" — there is no longer a crumb on the altar that we can call bread or a drop we can call wine. These elements have become the Body and Blood of Jesus. His presence, from then on, is real. Jesus is present with His Body, Blood, Soul, and Divinity.

Some of Jesus' early followers called this doctrine a "hard saying" (see John 6:60) and rejected it, but Jesus never backed down. Jesus' real presence is something we cannot see with our eyes, or taste or feel. Yet we can grow in our faith by studying and praying about these passages from the Bible:

- Matthew 26:26-28
- Mark 14:22-24

- Luke 22:19-20
- Luke 24:30-35
- John 6:25-65
- Acts 2:42, 46
- 1 Corinthians 11

For faithful Catholics, the Mass is more than a "service" or a "gathering":

- The Mass is the "re-presentation" of Jesus' sacrifice on the cross. On the cross, He poured out His blood and gave up His body. That event took place many years ago, but Jesus intended it for you and me, and so He left us the Mass. In the Mass, we join Him at Calvary.
- The Mass is how we share in the worship of heaven. The angels in heaven gaze upon God and worship before Him forever. In the Mass, we join in prayers with the angels and saints.
- It is our thanksgiving to God for all

He has given us. *Eucharist* means "thanksgiving" in Greek.

- It is Jesus Himself, really present as He promised. So it is also a peek ahead to His Second Coming at the end of time.

The Mass is the most powerful thing we will ever know. Yet we don't always get as much out of it as we would like. Here are some suggestions for improving the way we pray the Mass:

- **Try to get to Mass early.** It takes time for us to leave behind all the cares of the world. Once we've found our place in church, we should kneel for a moment and try to focus our thoughts on Jesus.
- **Try to go to Mass more than you have to.** All Catholics must go to Mass on Sundays and holy days of obligation. But most parishes offer Mass on weekdays

and Saturday mornings, too. Going to weekday Masses can help you improve the way you pray at Sunday Mass.

- **Dress up for the occasion.** People tend to dress up for important events (like weddings) and dress down for unimportant things (like games). What we wear can affect the way we think and feel. So, when we go to Mass, we should be clean, groomed, and respectably dressed.

- **Use a missal.** Most churches keep some sort of book or booklet in the pews so that people can follow along with the Mass. Some people find it helpful to read along as they listen to the prayers.

- **Make the responses.** It's not enough just to give our mind to the Mass. We have to give our *whole self*. God made us with a body and a soul so that we could use both to worship Him. The

Mass uses our voice in prayer and our body in gestures — standing, kneeling, and making the Sign of the Cross.

- **Sing the songs** — even if you can't carry a tune. We see in the Book of Revelation that the angels and saints sing around the throne of God in heaven. We on earth should do the same. St. Augustine said singing is like praying twice.

- **Learn the "parts" of the Mass.** The Mass is made up of several parts. It can be helpful to have two or three places where you always "check back in" if your mind has wandered:

    — *The "Lord, have mercy."* Here's a great time to tell God you're sorry — for gossiping, for lying, for eating too much, or whatever. Going to Mass and receiving Communion will wipe away all your venial sins.

— *The readings.* Try to focus on one thing God is trying to tell you in the day's readings.

— *The offertory.* When the priest brings the bread and wine to the altar, say a silent prayer to give God all your school work, friendships, sports and games, and family life. God will change our lives, then, as He changes the bread and wine into His Body and Blood.

— *Communion.* As you're walking back to your pew, remember that Jesus is within you now — the same Jesus Who died on a cross for you. Tell Him your worries, even if you're angry or sad. He is listening in love.

• **Be grateful.** Always take time to say "thank you" in the course of the Mass, especially after Communion.

WHY GO TO
CONFESSION?

Many people miss out on confession, not because they don't know how to go, but because they're afraid, or because they don't know what they're missing.

It's natural to fear confession if you don't go very often. The number of your sins, from many months or years, can seem huge. Maybe, too, you feel ashamed, and you dread talking about your sins. Maybe you're afraid of looking someone in the face as you tell your sins. (Most churches provide two ways to go to confession: face-to-face with the priest or behind a screen.)

But the best cure for this fear is just to dive right in. Find out what time your parish offers confession, then examine your conscience, and go.

If you haven't been to confession in a while, or if you're not sure how to begin, let the priest know. And if you're nervous, say so. The point of confession is mercy; so the more mercy the priest can dispense in the name of God, the happier the occasion should be.

The fear of confession will probably disappear if you make a habit of going. If you go at least once a month, to a priest you've chosen as your regular confessor, you'll get used to opening your soul to him.

If you avoid the sacrament of penance because you don't think your sins are serious enough, then you need to get to know yourself better. The Bible tells us, "If we say, 'We are without sin,' we deceive ourselves, and the truth is not in us" (1 John 1:8). The sacrament will help us to know ourselves better. When we speak our sins aloud, God helps us see our faults more clearly.

Confession is the ordinary way that Jesus gave us to make our lives right with God and with the Church. He gave His first priests the power to forgive sins in His name, and His priests continue that work today. In the sacrament, God Himself forgives us. God heals your soul when the priest says, "I absolve you. . . ."

HOW TO MAKE A GOOD CONFESSION

Confession is not difficult, but we *do* need to prepare for it. We should begin with prayer, placing ourselves in the presence of God. Then we should try to review our lives since our last confession, searching out our thoughts, words, and actions that did not measure up to God's love, His law, or the laws of the Church. Reviewing our life this way is called an "examination of conscience," and it is a good thing to do every day (see Page 95).

Once you get to the confessional, follow these four steps to make a good confession:

1. **Tell all.** Try not to leave out any serious sins. Start with the one that is toughest to say.

2. **Be clear.** Try not to hide things or make them sound better.

3. **Be sorry.** Remember, it is God you have offended, and it is His forgiveness you seek.

4. **Be brief.** No need to go into detail. Often when we do, we are just trying to excuse ourselves.

THE RITE OF
RECONCILIATION

After the customary greetings, the penitent crosses himself:

> *In the name of the Father, and of the Son, and of the Holy Spirit. Amen.*

The priest urges the penitent to have confidence in God. The priest may say:

> *May the Lord be in your heart and help you to confess your sins with true sorrow.*

Either the priest or the penitent may read or say by heart some words taken from the Holy Scripture about the mercy of God and repentance, for example:

> *"Lord, You know all things; You know that I love You"* (John 21:17).

The penitent tells his or her sins. The priest gives opportune advice, imposes the penance, and invites the penitent to make known his or her contrition. The penitent may say, for example:

Lord Jesus, Son of God, have mercy on me, a sinner.

Or the penitent may pray the Act of Contrition found on Page 70.

The priest gives absolution:

God, the Father of mercies, through the death and resurrection of His Son has reconciled the world to Himself and sent His Holy Spirit among us for the forgiveness of sins; through the ministry of the Church, may God give you pardon and peace, and I absolve you from your sins in the name of the Father, and of the Son, and the of the Holy Spirit.

The penitent answers: *Amen.*

The priest dismisses the penitent with this prayer or one like it:

May the Passion of Our Lord Jesus Christ, the intercession of the Blessed Virgin Mary and of all the saints, whatever good you do and suffering you endure heal your sins, help you to grow in holiness, and reward you with eternal life. Go in peace.

The penitent should fulfill the penance imposed without delay.

HOW TO MAKE AN EXAMINATION OF CONSCIENCE

In an examination of conscience, we try to see our day as God sees it. It is a review of our day's events, measuring our thoughts, words, and deeds against the moral law and the demands of the Christian vocation. The practice enables us to see our faults and root them out with God's help.

To make an examination of conscience, we should:

1. Begin by recalling that we are in God's presence.
2. Consider our day's events, referring to questions we have prepared. (For examples, see below.)
3. Tell God we are sorry for our sins.
4. Promise to try not to sin again.

Some Suggested Questions

- Do I pray to God every day? Do I pray for my family and friends?
- Have I thanked God for His gifts to me?
- Am I attentive at Mass? Do I receive Communion with care and attention?
- Have I worked unnecessarily on Sunday?
- Have I missed attending Mass on Sundays or holy days of obligation?
- Have I spoken God's name in disrespectful ways?
- Have I respected and obeyed my elders, parents, employers, or teachers?
- Have I harmed other people through acts of violence or neglect?
- Have I been rude or impatient?
- Have I taken anything that I had no right to take?
- Have I taken school supplies?
- Have I shared all that I should — of my belongings, my time, my friendship?

- Have I treated other people's property carelessly?
- Have I said things that I knew would hurt someone?
- Have I gossiped?
- Have I lied?
- Have I emphasized the negative qualities of other people?
- Have I spoken badly of the Church?
- Have I boasted about myself or my work?
- Have I been dishonest — with my teachers, my family, or anyone else?
- Have I placed false information on forms or in reports in school?
- Is there anyone I have made to feel unwelcome in my presence?
- In my thoughts or glances, have I invaded anyone's privacy in a way that would make them hurt or uncomfortable if they knew?
- Have I used well the time and talents God has given me?

- Have I offered my classmates, friends, and family a good example of Christian life? Do I speak to them about God and offer to pray with them or for them?
- Do I tell people how much I appreciate them?
- Do I pray every day that friends and family members who have died may now rest in peace?
- Are there people I have refused to forgive?
- Do I dress modestly?
- Have I envied other people for the things they own or the friends they have?

THE CHURCH CALENDAR AND THE SAINTS

The Church year is divided into seasons, which include special times such as Easter, Lent, Christmas, and Advent. Each of these focuses on a particular mystery of the life of Jesus. There are also thirty-three or thirty-four weeks every year called "Ordinary Time." During Ordinary Time, the Church celebrates the mystery of Christ in its fullness. On particular days each year, we remember the saints and angels who have played important roles in God's work.

Some saints are honored as "patron saints," who dedicate their prayer in heaven to specific concerns of people on earth.

Advent

Advent begins the Church year. It is the time of waiting, hoping, and preparation before Christmas, normally beginning with the first Sunday in December. Advent means "coming" and refers to Jesus' birth in Bethlehem, His presence to us today in the sacraments and in other people, and His future coming at the end of time.

December 6
St. Nicholas, Bishop of Myra
(died around the year 350)

Nicholas lived in what is now Turkey. He inherited great wealth when his parents died, but he used his money to help others. The stories about Bishop Nicholas's generosity to the poor and his love of children have inspired Christians for many generations.

December 8
The Immaculate Conception
(holy day of obligation)

This is the day we celebrate God's singular gift to Mary. From the first moment of her being, God filled Mary with all grace and holiness, and He preserved her from sin throughout her life. Under the title of "the Immaculate Conception," Mary was declared the Patroness of the United States.

December 12
Our Lady of Guadalupe

In December 1531, in Mexico, Our Lady appeared to an Aztec man named Juan Diego. Her message to him inspired the conversion of millions of people in that land. Her image appeared miraculously on Juan Diego's cloak, where it remains even today.

December 25
Christmas
(holy day of obligation)

This is the day we celebrate Jesus' birth. The greatest wonder of all time is that God became a man in Jesus Christ. He entered history in order to save us. We give gifts to recall God's finest gift to us.

December
(Sunday After Christmas)
The Holy Family

We honor Jesus with His earthly parents, Mary and Joseph. The Scriptures teach us that human love and family life are holy and can lead us to heaven.

January 1
Mary, Mother of God
(holy day of obligation)

Mary is the mother of Jesus, Who is both God and man. We honor her with the title "Mother of God." Her family relationship with God was special, and it gave her a special family bond with us. Because we are brothers and sisters of Christ, God's mother is our mother, too.

January
(Sunday After New Year's Day)
Epiphany

On Epiphany, we celebrate the way God has shown Himself to the world. Wise men from the East followed a star to Bethlehem, where they found Jesus with His mother. They gave Him precious gifts and showed Him their love and reverence.

January 4
St. Elizabeth Ann Seton
(1774-1821)

Elizabeth Seton was born into an upper-class Protestant family in New York. She married a wealthy businessman, with whom she had five children. Her husband died, however, when the children were young. Elizabeth converted to Catholicism, and she opened a school to support her family. Eventually, she founded many schools and an order of sisters to teach in them.

January 5
St. John Neumann
(1811-1860)

John Neumann was born in Bohemia. There were too many priests in his home diocese. So, rather than wait to be ordained, he asked to be assigned as a missionary to German immigrants in the United States. Eventually, he was received into the Redemptorist order. He served in several cities and became bishop of Philadelphia. He founded many schools and an order of sisters. He died at the age of forty-eight, worn out from his work for God.

January
(Sunday After Epiphany)
The Baptism of the Lord

The Spirit descended upon Jesus when John baptized Him in the Jordan River. After His baptism, a voice said, "This is My beloved Son. My favor rests on Him" (Matthew 3:17). Through baptism, we share in Jesus' sonship. We are children of God, and we are called to follow His way of holiness and service to others.

January 18-25
Church Unity Octave

This is an eight-day period when we pray for peace within the Church and reunion with other Christians who are separated from the Catholic Church.

February 2
The Presentation of the Lord

Mary presented her Son, Jesus, in the Temple with the customary sacrifice prescribed by their religion. On this day, the Church blesses candles for use at Mass and in homes. Sometimes called "Candlemas," this feast celebrates Jesus as the Light of the World.

February 3
St. Blaise
(died around the year 316)

The Church blesses throats today as a holy prevention against diseases of the throat. A martyr of the early Church, St. Blaise was said to have healing power. We recognize the power of those who have given themselves entirely to Jesus.

February 11
Our Lady of Lourdes

This feast celebrates the tenderness of God's mother, the Virgin Mary, for all of us on earth and focuses on an important aspect — her Immaculate Conception. In 1858, Our Lady appeared to fourteen-year-old Bernadette Soubirous, as she and two companions gathered firewood. Our Lady appeared to her eighteen times. During the sixteenth visit, Our Lady identified herself as the Immaculate Conception. After four years of investigation, the Church finally stated that Bernadette's claims were credible and that Our Lady had appeared to her.

Lent
Ash Wednesday

Ash Wednesday is the beginning of Lent. The Church marks our foreheads with ashes to remind us that some day we will die. With that in mind, we begin a period of forty days of intense effort to change our lives — and to begin living for a life that will last, even when our bodies are "dust and ashes." The Church celebrates Lent as a time of conversion and a preparation for Easter. During Lent, we try to be more like Jesus, by praying and making sacrifices (like not eating meat on the Fridays of Lent, eating small meals on Ash Wednesday and Good Friday, and giving up sweets or limiting television viewing or video games). We should consider giving our time or money to charity or to those less fortunate. Lent is also a time to think about Jesus' suffering and death.

March 17
St. Patrick
(389-461)

Patrick rose from slavery to become a priest, a bishop, and the man most responsible for converting Ireland from paganism. He was a man of action. In less than thirty years of ministry, he managed to bring the whole island over to Christianity. He did all this in spite of his lack of education and his disadvantaged youth. Patrick wrote beautiful works about the Faith, which are still read and prayed today. He is the Patron of Ireland.

March 19
St. Joseph

The Bible pays Joseph a high compliment, saying that he was a "just" (or "righteous") man (see Matthew 1:18-25). That means he was open to doing all that God wanted. God paid Joseph a higher compliment by choosing him to be the husband of Mary and foster-father to Jesus. He cared for the Holy Family, fleeing with them to Egypt when they were in danger. He later brought them back to Nazareth, where he supported them with his work and taught Jesus a trade. On May 1, the Church celebrates the feast of St. Joseph the Worker.

March 25
The Annunciation

In the middle of Lent falls the great feast of the Annunciation. We recall that Mary received word from the angel Gabriel that she would bear the Son of God in her womb. In that story, Tradition found the words of the Hail Mary.

Holy Thursday

We remember the Last Supper, when Jesus celebrated the first Mass and established His priesthood.

Good Friday

We remember the day when Jesus was crucified and died in order to save us.

The Easter Vigil

This is the night before Easter, when the Church celebrates new life through the resurrection of Jesus. This is the usual time for new Catholics to be received into the Church.

Easter

We remember and celebrate that Jesus rose from the dead, and now He lives forever. By rising, He conquered death for all of us. In His resurrection, we find our hope for our own future. We, too, will one day rise, with our bodies, to enjoy life forever. The Easter Triduum — extending from Holy Thursday to Easter Sunday — is the high point of the Church year. What Sunday is to the week, Easter is to the year. Easter is the most important day in the entire Church calendar.

The Ascension
(holy day of obligation)

Forty days after His resurrection on Easter, Jesus blessed His apostles and ascended to glory in heaven.

Pentecost

Fifty days after Easter, the apostles gathered in one room. They were filled with the Holy Spirit, as Jesus had promised. The Holy Spirit gave them courage to spread the Gospel. Pentecost is sometimes called "the birthday of the Church."

May 31
The Visitation

In response to the angel Gabriel's message, Mary set out to visit her cousin Elizabeth, who was also expecting a baby and needed help. Elizabeth greeted her visitor with "Blessed are you among women, and blessed is the fruit of your womb" (Luke 1:42). Elizabeth's baby was St. John the Baptist.

June 3
St. Charles Lwanga and Companions
(died 1885-1887)

One of 22 Ugandan martyrs, Charles died rather than take part in sinful and impure actions. While in prison, he instructed his friends in the Catholic Faith.

July 14
Blessed Kateri Tekakwitha
(1656-1680)

Kateri was the daughter of a Mohawk chief who lived first in the state of New York and later in Quebec, Canada. When she was only four, both of her parents died of smallpox. She, too, caught the illness, which left her with impaired vision. She was baptized a Christian and chose not to marry in order to consecrate herself entirely to God.

August 15
The Assumption
(holy day of obligation)

At the end of her days on earth, Mary was taken, body and soul, into heaven. God did this to show us that, one day, we, too, would live with Him in our glorified bodies.

September 8
The Birth of Mary

Mary was brought into the world in a unique way. From the moment of her conception, she had all holiness and suffered none of the weaknesses that come from original sin. God kept her pure and holy, beautiful and glorious, to be the mother of His Son, Jesus. Sts. Anne and Joachim were her parents.

September 27
St. Vincent de Paul
(1580-1660)

Vincent grew up in a large French peasant family. As a boy, he cared for the family's farm animals. He saw the poverty of his fellow parishioners and was moved to help them. Vincent had many wealthy and powerful friends, but he loved the poor. He started a religious order and parish groups to help the poor. Today the St. Vincent de Paul Society is active all over the world.

September 29
Sts. Michael, Raphael, and Gabriel

Stories of these three archangels are found in the Scriptures. The prophet Daniel mentions St. Michael, the heavenly prince who stands guard over God's people and leads the heavenly powers against Satan. The Bible's Book of Tobit tells the story of Raphael, who accompanied Tobit's son, Tobiah, on a mission of mercy and helped him find a wife. He is considered the Patron of Travelers. Luke's Gospel shows Gabriel as the angel who appeared to Mary and asked her to become the mother of Jesus.

October 1
St. Thérèse of the Child Jesus
(1873-1897)

All her life, Thérèse suffered from illness. She sometimes even feared she would lose her faith. A French Carmelite nun, she chose hidden sacrifices over public works. "I prefer the monotony of obscure sacrifice to all ecstasies," she said. "To pick up a pin for love can convert a soul." She died at age 24. She is the Patroness of the Missions and is honored as a Doctor (or Teacher) of the Church.

October 2
Guardian Angels

A day for renewing friendships and deepening them with the dear, gentle, unintrusive spirit who watches over us night and day.

October 4
St. Francis of Assisi
(1182-1226)

The son of a rich Italian merchant, Francis spent his youth in a carefree way. Then serious illness brought him to realize the emptiness of his ways, and Francis made a spiritual turnaround. Yet he remained a happy soul with a song ever on his lips. He founded the Franciscan order of priests, brothers, and sisters. Francis received the *stigmata*, the marks of the wounds of Christ in his hands, feet, and side.

October 7
Our Lady of the Rosary

The Rosary is one of the most beloved Catholic prayers. It is addressed to Mary and focuses on the events in the life of her Son, Jesus. It has been recommended by saints and popes for centuries.

October 15
St. Teresa of Ávila
(1515-1582)

Teresa was a Spanish Carmelite nun who spoke in familiar, loving conversation with Jesus. By her example, her prayers, and her hard work, she reformed her order of nuns and inspired many women to follow her way of life. Teresa's writings give much good advice about prayer. She is a Doctor of the Church.

October 19
Sts. Isaac Jogues,
John de Brebeuf, and Companions
(died 1642-1649)

Jesuit missionaries from France, Isaac and his companions became the first Catholics to die as martyrs on the North American continent. They gave up their careers in France to work among the Hurons and

Iroquois in the New World. A hostile tribe beat, tortured, and killed these missionaries along with their Huron converts.

November 1
All Saints
(holy day of obligation)

The Church honors not only the saints who are canonized, but the many who lived quiet lives on earth before passing into glory in heaven. The saints in heaven may include members of our family and even friends of ours who have died. They, too, can pray for us before the throne of God.

November 2
All Souls

On this day, we remember those who have died and are still undergoing a cleansing that prepares them for heaven. This cleansing is called "purgatory." The Bible tells us it is a "holy

and wholesome thought to pray for the dead"
(2 Maccabees 12:45-46).

November 3
St. Martin de Porres
(1579-1639)

A Panamanian, Martin became a Dominican lay brother. At a young age, he learned medicine and surgery. He nursed the sick of his city and helped found an orphanage and hospital for children. He died of an illness he caught while serving the poor.

November 13
St. Frances Xavier Cabrini
(1850-1917)

When she was a child in Italy, Frances wanted to be a missionary to China. Instead, she came to the United States and cared for Italian immigrants. She built hospitals, schools, and orphanages. Frances was the first naturalized United States citizen to be canonized.

November 21
The Presentation of Mary

The parents of Mary brought her to the Temple in Jerusalem when she was three years old and dedicated her to God.

The Fourth Thursday of November
Thanksgiving Day

Though not officially a feast day of the Church, it still should be a time when we thank God for all His gifts to us.

November
(The Last Sunday in Ordinary Time)
Christ the King

Victorious over death, Christ rules heaven and earth. We honor Him as King of our lives as we end another Church year.

THOUGHTS ON CHRISTIAN FRIENDSHIP

"I call you friends."

— Jesus (John 15:15)

"Love one another as I have loved you."

— Jesus (John 15:12)

"There is no greater love than this, to lay down one's life for one's friends."

— Jesus (John 15:13)

"Let us show a friend our heart, and he will open his to us. . . . A friend, if he is true, hides nothing."

— St. Ambrose of Milan

"Rebukes are often better than silent friendship."

— St. Ambrose of Milan

"There is no greater invitation to love than loving first."

— *St. Augustine*

"Among our worst enemies are people destined to be our friends."

— *St. Augustine*

"True friendship should never conceal what it thinks."

— *St. Jerome*

"Friendships begun in this world will be taken up again, never to be broken off."

— *St. Francis de Sales*

ABOUT THE
AUTHORS

Father Kris D. Stubna received his doctorate in theology from the Pontifical Gregorian University in Rome. He is the editor of *The Catholic Vision of Love*, the most complete chastity education program based on authoritative documents of the Church. He is also the diocesan secretary for education for the Diocese of Pittsburgh.

Mike Aquilina is a prolific author in the Catholic press, the editor of *New Covenant* magazine, and the author, editor, or co-editor of several Our Sunday Visitor books including *The How-To Book of Catholic Devotions*, *The Mass of the Early Christians*, and *Weapons of the Spirit*.

Our Sunday Visitor . . .
Your Source for Discovering the Riches of the Catholic Faith

Our Sunday Visitor has an extensive line of materials for young children, teens, and adults. Our books, Bibles, booklets, CD-ROMs, audios, and videos are available in bookstores worldwide.

To receive a FREE full-line catalog or for more information, please call **Our Sunday Visitor** at **1-800-348-2440**. Or write, **Our Sunday Visitor**, 200 Noll Plaza, Huntington, IN 46750. Our website is **www.osv.com**.

- -

Our Sunday Visitor
200 Noll Plaza
Huntington, IN 46750
Toll free: **1-800-348-2440**
E-mail: osvbooks@osv.com
Website: www.osv.com